Jesus' First 100 Days of Ministry

(and why they matter)

John Pace

Author: John Pace

Date Published: January 14, 2017

ISBN: 978-0-9986221-1-8

Publisher: Crimson House Ministries

Copyright © Crimson Houses Ministries 2017

Unless otherwise noted, all scripture references are from the King James version of the Bible.

CRIMSON HOUSE MINISTRIES

All enquiries via www.crimsonhouseministries.org

Contents

Author's Note

I was fortunate to come across Michael Rood's *The Chronological Gospels* as a resource in a recent sermon series and was blessed by the knowledge of how Jesus operated day by day. It brought me a refreshing understanding of Jesus' lifestyle and an encouraging pattern to follow in His 'line upon line' teaching. My goal in writing this book is to simply share with you the blessings I have received, and the principles the Holy Spirit has revealed, in my study of Jesus' first 100 days (or so) of ministry. I will be using Jesus' baptism in the Jordan as His ministry's outset (Matthew 4:1-11) to the healing of the nobleman's son as recorded in John 4:44-54 as the 100-day window.

This work is relatively short by intention. It is not written as an academic thesis with multiple supporting evidences. Rather, it is a concise work that hopes to either: 1) confirm, solidify, and distill the personal knowledge and experience of the seasoned pastor; or 2) quicken, enlighten, inspire, and direct those new to their pastoral journey.

May you find this a read worthy of your time and the principles applicable to your ministry.

John Pace
January 2017

Preface

A notion that warped into reality—the importance of the first 100 days—started with Franklin D. Roosevelt's presidency. The term was coined in a July 24, 1933, radio address by U.S. President Franklin D. Roosevelt, although he was referring to the 100-day session of the 73rd United States Congress between March 9 and June 17, rather than the first 100 days of his administration.[1] However, the idea that a president's first 100 days are significant eventually arose from that reference right into FDR's presidency, "as he pushed through a flurry of bills during the Great Depression. Ever since, presidents have been judged against that useful, if somewhat arbitrary, benchmark."[2]

As ministers of the gospel and co-laborers with the Holy Spirit, we know that natural benchmarks don't necessarily apply in our spiritual settings. Yet, what if some of these natural benchmarks like the first 100-days have an unwitting root in spiritual principles? What if there is an underlying spiritual truth to this 100-day idea that is hidden from the natural man? While such a revelatory discussion maybe a worthy topic, I make no attempt to justify these principles in the natural. Rather, this is an honest interpretation of seven truths seen in Jesus' first 100 days of ministry. They are foundational in any new opportunity for leadership. Thus, the natural thought of a leader's first 100 days did not influence this writing; rather, it was the ultimate spiritual Being, Christ Jesus, who set the standard and then, in turn, influenced the natural belief.

In fact, any possible spiritual influence impacting the 100-day mentality is moot because the natural business/political world has perverted the Messiah's first 100-day model. How? By focusing on the immediate rather than the long-term; where instant results supersede the wisdom of a proper foundation for actions that will be bring strong results for years to come. President Lyndon B. Johnson gave us an example of this skewed, result-oriented mentality and the need to act quickly after his 1964 reelection victory: "I was just elected president by 15 million votes. Just by the natural way people think and because Barry Goldwater scared hell out of them, I have already lost about 2 of these 15 million and am probably getting down to 13. If I get in any fight with Congress, I will lose another couple of million, and if I have to send any more of our boys to Vietnam, I may be down to 8 million by the end of the summer."[3]

Certainly, looking naturally through a result-oriented lens, the Lord's first 100 days was far from stellar as He hadn't even put together His entire team of 12 by then; yet, no one can honestly argue that the lasting effect of those first 100 days are unprecedented as 2000 years later what Jesus started is still going strong. It is the goal of this book to equip the pastor of a new congregation with seven principles that will create, well beyond that first 100-day mark, a foundation that will uphold a strong and vibrant spiritual house for years to come. Therefore, "The first hundred days mark is not the end of the story, it's the end of the beginning. Leaders entering new roles can stumble badly and still recover. But it's a whole lot easier if they don't stumble in the first place. And that's why the transition period matters so much."[4]

---

[1]Alter, Johnathan The Defining Moment: FDR's Hundred Days and the Triumph of Hope (Simon and Schuster, 2007) p 273.

[2]Chung, Juliet, "History's Verdict: What 100 Days Can Reveal - WSJ," accessed October 10, 2015, http://www.wsj.com/articles/SB124096652262466393.

[3]Lesser, William, "First One Hundred Days," read October 10, 2015, http://college.cengage.com/polisci/resources/first_100_days/articles/critical.html.

[4]IBID.

Introduction

Fulfilling the Call

As genuine God-called ministers, you, I, and the Apostle Paul have at least one thing in common—it was the Lord who placed that in us. When Jesus ascended on high, He gave gifts unto men. As a recipient of a 5-fold gift, you yourself are a two-fold gift: You are a beneficiary of the Lord's leadership gift; and you are a gift by the Lord to those He has placed before those you lead. But there is more.

"...I thank Christ Jesus our Lord, who hath enabled me, for that he counted me faithful, putting me into the ministry" (1 Timothy 1:12).

Not only are you a two-fold gift of God, you are counted faithful. Yes, you are counted faithful. And not just faithful, but enabled as well. Kenneth Wuest defines the key words in this First Timothy passage so beautifully (sentences in italics are my emphasis):

o "The word "enabled" is *endunō*. Paul uses this verb in Philippians 4:13, "I am strong in the sphere of all things in the One who is constantly infusing strength in me." *Paul thus was clothed with the ability to proclaim the good news of salvation.*

o   The word "counted" is *hēgeomai*, "to deem, account, consider, think." It refers to a deliberate and careful judgment. God saw that the fiery, zealous, intense Pharisee would be just as fiery, zealous, and intense in the proclamation of the gospel as he was in its persecution, when saving grace was operating in his being.

o   God demonstrated His confidence in Paul by putting him into the ministry. The participle is aorist, its classification, circumstantial. *God considered Paul trustworthy, having put him into the ministry.*

o   The word *diakonia* means "service, ministering." It speaks of a branch of activity [as in the military] in which the individual renders service. Here it is Christian service. The word "ministry" today is used of the ordained clergy. Paul thought of the sphere of Christian service as a whole. God placed him in the service."[5]

You, my friend, have been found faithful—trustworthy— and the Lord of Hosts has put you into Christian service, whether it is ordained ministry (the focus of this book) or a marketplace missionary (see my Shepherds of the Lost series for more on this). By His amazing grace your worldly passions and zeal have been translated from the kingdom of darkness to the kingdom of light; you have been strengthened to proclaim His glorious gospel. Praise God for His faithfulness and trust in you! And now, you are looking at that first 100 days in a new place of Christian service and want to set a solid foundation.

The Importance of the First 100 Days

Let us consider this quote from the business world: "So the first 100 days are important for many reasons, they are periods of great opportunity but also risk, actions or decisions taken in this period can have far reaching consequences, they establish a foundation or momentum for the new leader and lastly they are not once offs, i.e. most of us will make multiple transitions in our careers."[6]

I want to target two noteworthy ideas from Gillen's quotation: 1) establishing a foundation and 2) our first 100 days will be experienced more than once. In 32 years of ministry, I have had at least eight major first 100 days opportunities (three pastorates and five denominational positions)—and comparatively speaking, I thought I was relatively stationary since of those eight, only four involved new city/state relocations. The great majority of pastors are not so fortunate. Depending on the source, the average tenure of a pastor in America ranges anywhere from 30 to 48 months.[7] With a median tenure of 39 months as taken from the average pastoral residency, the minister would have nearly ten first 100 days, and many times in ten different cities.

There are multiple reasons for a pastor's relocation; yet, even in that multiplicity, the pastor can lay a consistent foundation at each church that can either propel them well beyond the average tenure or bring a personal contentment of consistency and integrity as they move to shepherd another congregation.

The Chief Shepherd gave us seven principles in His first 100 days of ministry to model in building our foundation and they will be used consistently in as many locations He may send us. Again, beginning Jesus' ministry with His baptism in the Jordan, we will see the following principles and their Scripture references:

1. Staying True to Who You Are (Matthew 4:1-11);

2. Selecting Trustworthy Individuals (John 1:29-51);

3. Establishing Authority (John 2:1-11);

4. Upending the Status Quo (John 2:13-25);

5. Modus Operandi—The Holy Spirit (John 3:1-21);

6. The New Focus (John 4:1-43);

7. Reaffirmation (John 4:44-54).

As we begin to expound these principles in the following chapters let us not be a '100-day hard-liner,' where every principle must be experienced to its fullest and completed by that concluding day, because that may not be accurate. True however, though maybe only introduced in those first 100 days, is that these seven principles will be in play throughout your pastorate as you build on that foundation.

––––––––

[5]Wuest, Kenneth Samuel, Wuest's Word Studies from the Greek New Testament: For the English Reader, 3 vols. (Grand Rapids, Mich.: Eerdmans, 1973).

[6]Gillen, Kevin, "Why Are the First 100 Days so Important?" accessed October 10, 2015, http://tweakyourbiz.com/management/2010/02/03/why-are-the-first-100-days-so-important/.

[7]http://www.churchlendersdirectory.com/pastoralturnoverarticle.html; http://www.namb.net/namb1cb1col.aspx?id=8590001122

1—Staying True to Who You Are

"If thou be the Son of God…" (Matthew 4:3)

Forty of the Lord's first 100 days were spent in prayer and fasting…and temptation. The first 40 days of His ministry were spent in solitude. There were no Bible studies, no worship services, no sermons to prepare for, no vision or mission statements, and no members to meet. There was only private prayer and fasting.

But there was something that did take place within those first 40 days of the Lord's first 100: He stayed true to who He was. The Tempter came at Him time and time again, trying to have Jesus exercise His Eternal Godhood as the Son of God to satisfy his earthly needs as the Son of Man. But Jesus stayed true as the Son of Man; indeed, He was tempted in all points as we are and was without sin.

God is Spirit; yet, with the incarnation God, in Christ Jesus, became body, soul, and spirit. And the adversary was going to appeal to each part of triune man in his attempt to defeat God's will for man. Satan's attacks were not new. They were the same as in the Garden of Eden. "And when the woman saw that the tree was good for food (a temptation of the body), and that it was pleasant to the eyes (a temptation of the soul), and a tree to be desired to make one wise (a temptation of the spirit—'you shall be as gods,' the adversary said), she took of the fruit thereof, and did eat, and gave also unto her husband with her; and he did eat" (Genesis 3:6).

Following Satan's success with the first Adam, the battle plan was the same for the Second: a tempting of body, soul, and spirit. The adversary's theme was the same, only the script had been altered. His temptation of the body moved from fruit for food in the Garden to "make these stones bread" in the wilderness; his temptation of the soul (the seat of man's will and emotions) of a fruit pleasing to the eyes became the fruit of pride in "cast yourself down, for God will give His angels charge concerning thee"; and the desire to be reverenced with God-like wisdom became, "All these things will I give thee, if thou wilt fall down and worship me" (Matthew 4:9).

Yet in the most trying of circumstances Jesus stayed true to Himself; He stayed true to God's plan for Him. He countered each temptation with what would become, for us, the sword of the Spirit—the word of God. And in that victory, He secured our salvation and your calling!

Your First 40 Days

Can you imagine the first Sunday at your new church using Jesus' model literally? "Um," the moderator would hesitantly open with as he stands behind the pulpit. "We would like to welcome our new pastor today...but, um, he is out on a fast and won't be here for six weeks," his eyes would nervously dart around the congregation. "Oh, but please continue to give as the offering plate comes your way, because we still need to support our pastor." Yes, such a beginning could make it your shortest pastorate of your ministry.

Without a doubt, few churches would embrace such a beginning, but I honestly wonder just how things would be if your first 40 days were spent that way. Instead of such a drastic introduction, most of us will need to experience and establish this first principle of staying true to our self, not just in private, but also in the wilderness of the congregation.

Temptation One

Like both Adams before you, rest assured that you too will be tempted in body, soul, and spirit. So many times, the adversary will begin first with your physical needs, 'bread' as it were. Maybe you left a comfortable lifestyle in suburban America, living the American dream in obeying the call of God, or maybe you have just graduated from Seminary, academically prepared for a lifestyle of obeying the call. But now you're six weeks in, the dream has become a nightmare, and school's preparation doesn't put food on the table.

And then here comes the adversary: "If you are a son of God you have physical needs which must be met. Here's the logical way of meeting those needs."[8] And instead of trusting the One who has secured our eternity, we trust our self in meeting our needs. But from that seed comes a tree of selfishness. Those who succumb to this bodily temptation ultimately become worldly ministers living for creature comforts, and they are constantly on the lookout for the dollar.

Know that the adversary will come with his first attack of physical needs. But resist him and battle him with the sword of the Spirit, "Therefore take no thought, saying, What shall we eat? or, What shall we drink? or, Wherewithal shall we be clothed? (For after all these things do the Gentiles seek) for your heavenly Father knoweth that ye have need of all these things" (Matthew 6:31-32). Trust the Father and let Him be your provider.

Temptation Two

With the use of Scripture in Satan's second temptation, he will come at a minister tempting him with the unholy desire of a super-spiritual attitude and that of 'spiritual' stardom.

"Go to the pinnacle of the temple, go to where everyone will see you, and show just how much God is with you" can be Satan's script for you. "Have your revival miracles be more outrageous than the previous one, so that everyone knows God is with you" he would continue. And yes, you have anointing; and yes, God is with you; and yes, it is evident that He is working—but it is for His glory and not yours.

This is such a mega temptation in western Christianity where the business model of 'bigger is better,' flashy commercials, and self-promotion influence the church. But Jesus did not succumb to this temptation of soul. The emotion of self-importance and the pride of mass recognition and self-glory—notoriety—were refuted with the Word.

Bob Sorge writes, "One of the most insidious temptations for pastors and ministers, and something that has clawed to find a hold in my soul, is the desire for notoriety. It flies under so many pious disguises: 'I want to be well-known so that my message will be received.' 'It's good for people to see my picture, because then they can get a sense of my spirit by the expression of my countenance.' 'I want to advertise our event in that Christian magazine so that we can touch more people with the power of Jesus Christ.' 'The more that people know about me and my ministry, the more the potential to change their lives.'

"Look at it carefully: The desire to cultivate a large following and have one's name become a household word is completely nonexistent in Jesus' life. Say it with me, 'In Jesus' name, I despise notoriety and the attention of men.'"[9] And speak the Word of the Lord, "Thou shalt not tempt the Lord thy God."

Temptation 3

The temptation of spirit came with the question, 'who will you worship?' as Satan said to Jesus, "…All these things will I give thee, if thou wilt fall down and worship me" (Matthew 4:9). And you will face the same temptation, maybe just not as blatantly asked.

Certainly, most ministers would never accept the idea of worshiping the Evil One; however, if any would pay homage to the world then isn't it the same? Sure, as the ruler of this world, Satan offered its glory—its reverence—to Jesus, if Jesus would worship him. Of course, we know by reading the Scripture that everything in heaven, and earth, and under the earth, will ultimately worship Jesus. So, what was the temptation? Would "Jesus respond to Satan's offer of a painless shortcut to world dominion, or [would] He choose the Father's road, the Calvary road?"[10].

The Lord has a perfect and complete plan for each one of us. The temptation is which road will we choose to attain the end result. Whose honor are we truly cultivating anyway? Is it the world's? Or the Lord's?

Pastors would do well to remember a small phrase in Genesis 46:34, "for every shepherd is an abomination unto the Egyptians." Even with what would seem like a proper motive, shaking hands and paying homage to the world will not bring eternal results to our witness. You will be hated, because Jesus was hated; you will be despised because those of this world love darkness rather than light.

Remember the first command, "Love God with all your heart, mind, soul, and spirit" and your worship will be pleasing to Him!

18

Summary

Know that you will be tempted early on to stay true to who you are.

There will be provisional and physical challenges (temptation for the body); there will be 'glory' temptations to your soul ('you are so much better than our former pastor'); there will be worship temptations to your spirit (which road are you going to take?).

Throughout His ministry, Jesus could have taken His provision into His own hands, but never once did He. In sharing with the scribes, He said, "'Foxes have holes, and birds of the air have nests, but the Son of Man has nowhere to lay his head'" (Matthew 8:20 ESV). He could have used his position to secure any place to call home, but He didn't. The provisional, take-it-in-your-own-hands trial is so strong that many fail to be content with the Father's provision. He knows what you have need of; yet, many times we never give Him the time to fill that need. Whatever may come your way, let the Provider be your source, He will always be on time—though it may not be when we think it should be.

Our souls will be tried with self-glory testing. When Jesus simply perceived that the crowds were going to make him king (cf. John 6:15) he withdrew Himself. And we must do the same, not physically per se, but with either an instruction, reproof, or rebuke to those who are trying to heap glory on us. And if we

19

find this desire clamoring within us remember the admonition, "Say it with me, 'In Jesus' name, I despise notoriety and the attention of men.'" Humble yourself with prayer and fasting, and let the Lord do the exalting, whether it is here and now, or on that great and wonderful Last Day.

The temptation to your spirit, the who-are-you-going-to-worship by which road you take, may be guised in sincerity, as with Peter's concern-based challenge to the Lord's future crucifixion: "And Peter took him aside and began to rebuke him, saying, 'Far be it from you, Lord! This shall never happen to you'" (Matthew 16:22 ESV). However, sincerity is not synonymous with truth and what Jesus heard in Peter's plea was the theme of Satan's third temptation—take my road and not Calvary's. Don't look for any shortcuts to fulfill the Lord's perfect will for your life, each of us have a 'Calvary road' on which we bear our cross. And it won't be the easy way of the adversary.

Finally, know that even though you are victorious in these temptations at the beginning, they will constantly return in hopes to make you be something other than who you are called to be. But whether it is in private times, where the adversary will speak seemingly convincing things to you, or when interacting with seasoned saints who want to nudge you their way, stay true to who you are. You are a child of the King; trustworthy and faithful you are: stay committed to Him and His way for you.

[8] Murphy, Edward F, The Handbook for Spiritual Warfare (Nashville: T. Nelson, 2003). Page 266.

[9] Sorge, Bob, In His Face: A Prophetic Call to Renewed Focus (Canandaigua, NY: Oasis House, 1994). Page 82.

[10] Murphy, page 268.

2—Selecting Trustworthy Individuals

"Follow me…" (John 1:43)

While there are some things that only you can do, you can't do everything by yourself. You must have trusted people around you. No, they won't be perfect; yes, they will make mistakes; and no, they won't do things just the way you would; in fact, one may even betray you, but you must have them. The wisdom of the Preacher speaks to such a need: "Two are better than one; because they have a good reward for their labour. For if they fall, the one will lift up his fellow: but woe to him that is alone when he falleth; for he hath not another to help him up. Again, if two lie together, then they have heat: but how can one be warm alone? And if one prevail against him, two shall withstand him; and a threefold cord is not quickly broken" (Ecclesiastes 4:9-12). Whether it is for a mistake that needs correcting, the warmth of encouragement, or withstanding a challenge, you need people around you…and you need to trust them.

Jesus, in the selecting of his first few disciples, gave us real direction in knowing how to choose those who will be close to us in our leadership. Granted, we don't have the luxury of being omniscient as He is, but there are several criteria we can glean from in His selection process. For Jesus, it began with His recognized authority; for you it begins with the recognized authority of Christ in you.

Behold, the Lamb

It is now day 40: Jesus is concluding His wilderness journey and staying true to His calling, staying true to who He is. John the Baptist, in the midst of his ministry, is experiencing the same temptation as priests and Levites from Jerusalem queried him with, 'Who are you' (cf. John 1:19). Like Jesus, John stays true to who he is, "I am the voice of one crying in the wilderness" (v. 23) is John's reply.

The next day, John sees Jesus and says, "Behold the Lamb of God that takes away the sin of the world" (v. 29). Then on the day after, "Again the next day after John stood, and two of his disciples; And looking upon Jesus as he walked, he saith, Behold the Lamb of God!" (John 1:35-36). Notice the difference in John's description of Jesus: the first time he speaks to Jesus' work; the second time he speaks to Jesus' person. It was the person the first two disciples followed, and then the work of God through the person. Jesus was going to make sure of that sequence with His first words, as recorded by John.

What Seek Ye

Just who were those two disciples who heard the Baptist's testimony and began to follow? Sure, we know their names— John and Andrew—but just who were they? Were they legalists looking to get in on the ground floor, or maybe even looking to sabotage the work? Were they ambitious time-servers seeking political advantage? Were they nationalists who wanted to ensure the status quo? Or maybe they were men who were of the 'right stuff.' After all, if the "followers of John were at all like himself, they were men who hungered and thirsted after real righteousness, being sick of the righteousness then in vogue."[11] Thus Jesus puts them to the test with three simple words, 'What seek thee?'

It wasn't "who do you seek?" but "what do you seek?" that He asked. Yet Jesus, all the while, desired their response to be based in who and not the what (cf. John 6:26, 27). And the two responded correctly, "Where dwellest thou?" (John 1:38) and then practically supported their answer, "and abode with him that day." Abode means to stay or dwell in a place, as it means in this passage. "A few times it means to last or continue, but more often it has a theological connotation to remain, continue, and abide."[12]

Jesus wanted disciples who would abide with Him, not just work with Him. In abiding with Him they would stay even when the work was difficult, extremely difficult. And though they might struggle even to the point of hiding, they would return— for there was nowhere else to turn. He wanted disciples who knew this was where they needed to be because He would lead them to where they, truly, always wanted to go.

What See Ye

It's a scriptural passage most everyone is familiar with: "...For the Lord sees not as man sees: man looks on the outward appearance, but the Lord looks on the heart" (1 Samuel 16:7 ESV). And with that understanding, Jesus gives us some insight as to just what to look for in selecting those who we select to lead with us.

With Peter and Nathaniel each had a unique backcloth to their selection—and one was not better than the other. In Peter, Jesus envisioned his potential; for Nathaniel, Jesus recognized his history. Thus, for one Jesus saw the future in selecting him and with the other, Jesus saw the integrity of his past in his choosing.

Picture Peter's face upon hearing the first words Jesus said to him, "...And when Jesus beheld him, he said, Thou art Simon the son of Jona: thou shalt be called Cephas, which is by interpretation, A stone" (John 1:42). Surely Peter's expression had to be one of astonishment and disbelief, so much so that he had nothing to say at the moment. But his demeanor would not deter the Lord. In fact, even through all of Peter's spiritual highs and lows, the Lord was not dissuaded from His choice. Jesus saw what Simon could be, a stone, and was committed to see him through, even with all the failures. Thus, it was a two-way street: Simon followed Jesus because of His person-hood; and Jesus committed to do the same with Simon.

Nathaniel, on the other hand, had a response to the Lord's introduction. "Whence knowest thou me," he said following the Lord's greeting of, "Behold an Israelite in whom there is no guile" (v. 47). Literally, Jesus' statement meant, behold, a "...true child of Israel after he had ceased to be the Supplanter."[13] Or in my way of thinking, an Israelite in whom there is no Jacob. Nathaniel was of Israel, but Israel was not in him. He was a man of character, not influenced by the world in which he lived, but by the convictions which he held. Nathaniel's personal history could easily transition to a Christ-filled futurity with his discipling by Jesus.

Summary

This work cannot be done alone; you must have others come beside you to accomplish everything that needs to be done. Rest assured there are others who long for a Christ-like leader; however, even with those who long for such you must still be discriminate in your selections. It just can't be anyone and it may not be the most obvious. The most important characteristic is their trustworthiness. A rationale for each choice may be different—from their history to the potential—but trustworthiness is the bedrock.

In fact, throughout your tenure you will need to select trustworthy individuals—Jesus started with five, added Matthew along the way, and then ordained all Twelve at the Sermon on the Plain (cf. Luke 6:12-16); He even added Paul after His resurrection. You too will do the same, and could even influence the selection of leaders after you've departed if your lifestyle, vision, and inspiration were both strong enough and accepted by others.

The initial key in selecting individuals is for those individuals to see Christ in you. They need to see that you are genuine; true to yourself in Christ Jesus. We will see in Principle 3 where followers will move from a recognized authority in you to an experienced authority with you, (and that too will need to happen at benchmark times of any leadership tenure). But before there is a commitment to you as their leader, before individuals will follow you and not simply engage in your work, they must see a personal integrity and humble confidence in you—a witness that comes only through your relationship with Christ.

Choosing trustworthy individuals who will follow the person and not the work will help 'weed out' those who simply want to use your experience as a step ladder without stepping up their own character. Don't misconstrue this 'follow the person' phrase with a cultish definition, but in the spirit of Scripture: "Those things, which ye have both *learned*, and *received*, and *heard*, and *seen in me*, do: and the God of peace shall be with you. (Philippians 4:9, *emphasis mine*). Hence, Paul's choice of words concerning Demas, "For Demas hath *forsaken me*, having loved this present world, and is departed unto Thessalonica; Crescens to Galatia, Titus unto Dalmatia. (2 Timothy 4:10, *emphasis mine*). With that understanding you and your trustworthy selections can abide together in the True Vine (John 15). For work isn't the reward for the vine, but the vine's bounty is fruitfulness. And we are called to be fruitful.

28

In making your selections, remember the words of the Lord, "…For the Lord sees not as man sees: man looks on the outward appearance, but the Lord looks on the heart" (1 Samuel 16:7 ESV). Your choices may meet resistance by the status quo—but you may see the historical integrity in a Nathaniel. They may question the wisdom of your choice of an unproven Simon—but you may see his potential. Commit to both in abiding together for what the Lord has called you to.

Finally, also realize that these trustworthy selections may not be with you until the end of your tenure; the Spirit may have other plans for them prior to your fulfillment. But rest assured, by abiding together, both of you will know the time and a possible departure will be blessed—both for the chosen who leaves and for the new selection God will give you.

––––––

[11] Bruce, Alexander B, The Training of the Twelve, Kindle Edition (Christian Classics Etheral Library, 2010).

[12] Walvoord and Zuck, J.F. and R.B., The Bible Knowledge Commentary: An Exposition of Scriptures, Logos Edition (Wheaton, Ill: Victor Books, n.d.).

[13] Vincent, Marvin, Vincent's Word Studies (Public Domain, 1886).

3—Establishing Spiritual Authority

"And his disciples believed on him" (John 2:11)

It is one thing to follow an individual and something entirely different to believe in them. In the last chapter, we saw where Jesus had followers, those who would 'be in the same way; that is, accompanying' Him[14] (cf. John 1:37,38, 40, 43). The first five did just that as they left where they were and followed Him some 20 miles from their initial encounter. It was there, at a common event and standing perfectly still physically, they moved from eager followers of Jesus to committed believers in Him: "...and his disciples *believed on* him" (John 2:11, *emphasis mine*). The definition of believed: "to have faith (in, upon, or with respect to, a person or thing), that is, credit; by implication to entrust (especially one's spiritual well-being to Christ)"[15].

Similarly, those trustworthy individuals you previously selected must make the transition from followers of you to believers in you. As followers, they saw something about you, a recognized authority that spoke to their soul. But when they experience with you an exercise of your anointed, spiritual authority, it will speak to their spirit. In so doing, in making that progression from followers of soul to believers in spirit, they will entrust you as their leader.

My Hour Has Not Yet Come

Jesus was simply responding to an invitation. He and His disciples were doing nothing more than going to enjoy the festive occasion at a wedding feast in Cana. Performing a miracle had to be the furthest thing from the Son of Man's mind. Yet, in the depths of the ceremony, He was put on the spot, His guest status challenged. "There is no more wine," His mother would tell Him. Can you imagine the thoughts racing through Jesus' mind as well as those following Him? No doubt there were many personal thoughts and theories as to what Jesus would do…if He could do anything. After all, we know that while He had unassumingly attended this wedding, He ended up displaying His spiritual authority to the glory of God.

That is the curiosity about establishing spiritual authority—you just don't set out to do it; hence Jesus' own witness of 'mine hour is not yet come' (cf. v. 4) It is just not a regular practice. You do not wake up one morning and say, "Today I am going to establish spiritual authority." Sure, there will be occasions that arise where you know spiritual authority will be exercised, but not so much established. In fact, those times of spiritual establishment will most generally happen spontaneously and when you least expect them—like when simply being a guest at a wedding.

Why spontaneous? Because genuine spiritual authority is a work of the Spirit and the Holy Spirit is the One who impresses such in the spirit of those trustworthy individuals following you.

It is in spontaneous moments where the 'real you' will be displayed. It is in those casual and unplanned moments when a submitted life to Christ will allow the Spirit to witness. It is in those impromptu situations where the spiritual leader lives out Christ's instruction to 'take no thought of what you will say, for the Holy Spirit will speak for you' (cf. Matthew 10:19). Whereas a carnal and calculating leader, one who relies on positional authority and is devoid of any fruit of the Spirit, cannot respond in the Spirit. This is why they will have followers—more likely position-seeking politicians and ladder-climbers—while you will have committed team leaders who trust in your leadership.

Knew Not Whence

Just like the Lord, your spiritual response in that spontaneous moment will be unknown to the masses, because the root of the response was not for them—although yes, they did enjoy its fruit—but rather it was intended for your selected ones. After tasting the water turned to wine, the masses were unaware of the miracle. In fact, we don't even know from the text whether or not the guests ever knew there was no wine, we only know that Mary commented on its absence and it was the bridegroom who was actually credited with providing the exquisite drink at the time.

But as mentioned above, this early establishment of spiritual authority was not for the masses but for the selected, and it was witnessed not just in the spiritual response, but in the love and humility with which it was done: love in how Jesus responded to

His mother's request, outside of His timing; humility in allowing the bridegroom credit and not drawing any attention to Himself.

Likewise, your trustworthy selections will move from following to entrusting, quietly and without the masses knowing, because they will know the real situation, the genuine and spiritual response, and the quickening in their spirit to your spiritual authority.

Summary

Early on there will be an occasion, nearly always unannounced and unplanned for, where you will have an opportunity to speak an inspired answer into someone's question. It may resolve a personally tabled inquiry that was always there, or perhaps answer an impromptu uncertainty and bring restful light to the asker's uneasy darkness. It may be spoken to a trustworthy member of your leadership team, or they may be witness to it; however, regardless of which, your team members, whether collectively or one-at-a-time, will be inspired to trust your leadership. They will move from one who follows you to one whom they entrust.

This transition won't be recognized by the masses, just as Jesus' miracle at the wedding wasn't grasped by the crowds. It will be, however, by the ones 'in the know,' as they are to be the true recipients of this moment.

This entrusting in your leadership can only be a work of the Spirit and is based in your Christian integrity and obedience. As you "follow after righteousness, godliness, faith, love, patience, meekness" (1 Timothy 6:11) your selected team of trustworthy individuals will follow after you.

In truth, such reestablishment will need to be continuing throughout your tenure (more on that in Chapter 7), though not as drastic as laying that initial 100-day foundation, and certainly not as spontaneous. As you and your team grow together in ministry, the team will need to regularly see that your inspiration is still there and that you are still following His leading. Paul constantly reestablished his leadership with in his team, as when he understood Agabus' prophecy in Acts 21 concerning him going to Jerusalem as preparation rather than avoidance.

Remember, you never want to become a 'yesterday's man' who lives off by-gone memories, decade-old testimonies, and ancient trust in days gone by; rather, always desire to be a 'today's man' who will inspire present-day leaders with freshly anointed leadership in a contemporary world needing a Savior.

----

[14] Strong, James, Strong's Hebrew and Greek Dictionaries (Public Domain, 1890).

[15] IBID

4—Upending the Status Quo

"…And overthrew the tables" (John 2:15)

There are those who have said that Isaac was the son of a great father (Abraham) and father to a great son (Jacob), but Isaac's adult life was relatively uneventful; certainly, one far from renown. Yes, he is in faith's 'hall of fame' (Hebrews 11), and was, obviously, faithful. But notice the writer's description of Isaac's faith, he blessed his sons "concerning things to come" (v. 20). Unlike Abraham, where the writer listed acts of faith, and Jacob whose current faith was presented (worshiped, v. 21), Isaac's faith was cast into the future. Isaac never really challenged the status quo; instead, he pretty much went with the flow.

There may be times in one of your ministry opportunities when you are called to simply go with the flow; God's plan for you during that particular tenure is an unassuming present, but a catalysis for the future, His desire is for your faith to be cast into the forthcoming. And that is good and fine and pleasing to the Lord. But most times you, in conjunction with the Spirit, will be the agent of change—the visible lighting rod in the tempest of upending the status quo. Just like Jesus was.

Make not my Father's House

For me, this is a most fearful phrase—"Make not my Father's house..." (John 2:16)—in what it doesn't plainly say: 'You have made my Father's house what you wanted and not what He desires.' That is the hazard of being creatures with freewill, people subject to like passions that battle the carnal nature and who have personal desires that are yet to be crucified in Christ.

Jesus faced such that day in the Temple as money-changers and merchandisers had made God's house into something it was never intended to be, and for a variety of reasons it had become the accepted norm. However, the status quo was about to change. The comfort, ease, and dishonor wrongfully given to the purpose and mission of the Temple was going to be upended as the tables were turned upside down.

The Temple cleansing—the upending of the status quo— became a benchmark moment in Jesus' ministry in His effort to restore the Temple to its original mission. The idea of Him destroying the Temple would resurface, and this benchmark at the beginning of His ministry would be referenced at the end of His tenure as well, and with all sorts of ramifications in between. It will be the same for you when you break up the status quo— the ease of Zion—as you are led by the Spirit.

Scripture, Signs, and Insight

Not everything is going to be immediately recognized as being a "God thing" when it is done, like with the Temple cleansing (cf. John 2:17). But if it's inspired by the Spirit through the Scripture, its purpose will eventually become known, as in the Temple being raised from the dead (cf. John 2:22).

Key in upending the status quo, first and foremost, is that it must be rooted in the Word; and even then, its timing must be inspired by the Spirit. Many 'up-endings' add an 'O' to the cause; that is, the idea may be right and go'o'd, but it is not God's time. However, when executed on God's time, whether immediately or any time after, His Word (and your rationale) will be revealed: "So shall my word be that goeth forth out of my mouth: it shall not return unto me void, but it shall accomplish that which I please, and it shall prosper in the thing whereto I sent it" (Isaiah 55:11). Such a revelation will be a sign of God's working with His people.

It must also be understood that upending the status quo could bring out the worst in people. Jesus' act of cleansing the Temple was met with hatred, jealousy, and godlessness, all of which ultimately resurfaced to testify at His death-penalty trial. Yet, it also launched something else that we must be ready to practice; an understanding that stands as the antithesis of selecting trustworthy men: "But Jesus did not commit himself unto them, because he knew all men, and needed not that any should testify of man: for he knew what was in man" (John 2:24-25).

Summary

That initial upending, your first big change to the status quo, will be a defining moment in your leadership tenure. Though certainly a weighty decision, it can't be neglected on the one hand, but neither can it be delayed on the other; and certainly, there is no need to change anything simply for the sake of change. It will need to be done and it will need to be in perfect harmony with the Holy Spirit. Your actions must be Scripture inspired and Spirit-timed and just because they are don't expect non-resistance. Dissent will surely come from some—and it will help you discern who not to trust at the time. But be assured, as change is rooted in the Word, your rationale for upending the status quo will come to light, not so much for personal satisfaction, but for the people to know God is working with them.

All of this change may need to come about in one (or more) of the following three main areas:

1. The mission of the institution;

2. The culture of your place of appointment;

3. The exchange of personnel and/or the excusing of others who willfully fight against you.

Let us first look at why a change in mission might be needful.

Every entity needs a mission statement. The Temple had a mission ordained by God as a place of presence, a place of prayer where God met with His people. The system for the mission had been in place for centuries; however, a system is only as reliable as the people who are in it. Thus, the Temple had lost its purpose for the sake of merchandise, and therefore, Jesus upended the status quo.

In turn, Jesus, as Head of the body, issued the church's mission with the declaration of the Great Commission. Once that Great Commission is embraced, then each local body will bring practical application to that mission. For example, a country church, suburban church, and an inner-city church will all make disciples, but how they specifically reach their part of the world will be based on local and people-needs.

However, over the course of time or by means of a weakness of flesh, the entity you are leading can come to arrive at the situation of the Temple in Jesus' day, turned into something other than originally intended. The Christ-called mission and work of the Spirit has been lost through programs, practices, and doctrines offered to edify the institution itself and please men. It is then that you will need to upend the status quo and bring the mission of the entity back to its original calling. And remember, it will most likely be met with resistance.

Secondly, while it may be that the mission has remained intact, perhaps it is the culture of your place of leadership that needs to be renewed. Jesus offered a change in culture when He gave the new command of 'love another' (cf. John 13:34, 35). A cold-blooded institutional climate where bricks, mortar, and institutional pride take precedent, as when the disciples marveled at the buildings (cf. Matthew 24:1), must be overturned to a culture of warm-blooded Christian love for all where a self-sacrificing life is the way of life: "Greater love has no one than this, that someone lay down his life for his friends" (John 15:13 ESV).

Paul reminded the church at Philippi of this self-sacrificing culture established by Jesus, "Do nothing from selfish ambition or conceit, but in humility count others more significant than yourselves. Let each of you look not only to his own interests, but also to the interests of others" (Philippians 2:3-4). Which practically means, "consider how you can help others, and in what way you can prosper them both in temporal things and in spiritual. You are members of a body, so one member is not to think for itself alone, the unity of the whole body requires that every separate and distinct part of it should be in harmony with the whole" (Spurgeon).

Finally, there may need to be a change in personnel; and that could be the actual, uncomplicated reason you are now in this location. With that, other changes in workers may need to take their place as you add to that beginning group of trustworthy individuals. This too can meet with resistance, but it will need to be done nonetheless. Paul and Barnabas had such a situation in their ministry team concerning John Mark. Note how Luke described the scenario: "And the contention was so sharp between them, that they departed asunder one from the other: and so Barnabas took Mark, and sailed unto Cyprus; and Paul chose Silas, and departed, being recommended by the brethren unto the grace of God" (Acts 15:39-40). Yes, such changes could get difficult.

However, needed changes in personnel that I find more troubling than difficult are those times when you need to excuse those who continually and willfully work to thwart your leadership. Obviously, we don't need to surround ourselves with 'yes men,' but those who won't agree to disagree in private meetings with you, who then leave that meeting and willfully work against you, need to be excused as divisions are sure to arise. There are also extreme cases where the adversary has influenced others to battle for control as in several of the seven churches of Asia—and it is so troubling when individuals allow carnal agendas and adversarial influences to manipulate them.

With all this before you, and the gravity in upending the status quo, remember the Lord's words to Joshua: "Have I not commanded you? Be strong and courageous. Do not be frightened, and do not be dismayed, for the LORD your God is with you wherever you go" (Joshua 1:9 ESV).

5—Modus Operandi, The Holy Spirit

"…born of flesh is flesh.. born of Spirit is spirit"
(John 3:6)

The need for Holy Spirit leading, guiding, and revelation
was emphasized heavily in the last chapter. It is interesting to
note that the Lord birthed the need of the Spirit within His first
100 days, not to His disciples directly, but to the Judean sage
Nicodemus.

Born of Flesh

'God is Spirit,' is what Jesus would later say to the woman at
the well; and His kingdom is like Him: spiritual. It was on day
57[16] of Jesus' first 100 that He introduced this understanding;
and it was not personally to His trustworthy selections (though
some were probably within ear-shot); rather, it was to the status
quo in the person of Nicodemus.

The status quo, as evidenced by the happenings at the
Temple, had fallen into a dull routine, presided over by worldly
men with a personal desire to get rich and exercise their
authority. But God's kingdom is anything but dull routine
marked by the unremarkable; conversely, it is a vibrant life-
giving realm that is constantly growing, and remarkably

changing—it is dynamically alive! But the status quo, steeped in the safety of the lethargic, can't grasp the challenge and discomfort of increase (at least not yet, as in Nicodemus' case); thus, the status quo will seek to destroy it. It is through the life-giving Spirit that status quo stagnation can be defeated.

Born of Spirit

Essentially what Jesus was saying to Nicodemus was 'like begets like;' that is, what is born of the flesh is flesh, but what is born of the Spirit is spirit. To live in God's kingdom, you must be born again; you must be born of the Spirit to be in the realm of His spiritual kingdom. That night the status quo failed to hear the words of Spirit, but what did not fail was Jesus laying the foundation of how things work in the kingdom: it is by and in and through the Spirit. You must be born again in every aspect of kingdom life, from the initial birth called salvation to the 'birthing' of every new direction and life-plan.

Born Again

The born-again experience is fundamental to the evangelical Christian. It is certainly nothing new. But here is the challenge in the modus operandi: Once inside the kingdom, new births must continue—not a repeat of the initial nativity that brought you into the kingdom—but all actions, vision, and understandings must be birthed of the Spirit to be genuine kingdom endeavors. They cannot be of the flesh. Even though they may sound good and seem correct in the natural, the flesh is not the matrix for the spiritual. The essential point is this: "...they that are in the flesh cannot please God" (Romans 8:8).

Just because we are in the kingdom through the new birth does not eliminate the flesh and blood of our bodies (as we saw in Chapter One). The truth is we will always have a wrestle of some sort between flesh and spirit until these corruptible bodies put on incorruption. None of us will be immune, and to think we ever get to 'that place' of immunity is a complete fallacy. The father of the faithful, Abraham, had an action of the flesh with the birth of Ishmael; Simon Peter had a fleshly vision lapse in backing down to a Jewish contingency regarding Gentile inclusion (cf. Galatians 2:2-13); and there were those in Paul's company who misunderstood the words of the Spirit in Agabus' prophecy (cf. Acts 21:10-14). Indeed, none of us are immune from our flesh.

Crucify the Flesh

It would be remiss to not mention briefly how to stay in the modus operandi: "And they that are Christ's have crucified the flesh with the affections and lusts: (Galatians 5:24). This crucifixion begins with salvation. "This initial act of faith in the Lord Jesus which resulted in the crucifixion (putting to death) of the affections and lusts of the totally depraved nature, is followed during the life of that Christian, by the free action of his liberated will in counting himself as having died to (having been separated from the power of) the evil nature with the result that he says NO to sin and stops yielding himself and his members to sin."[17] What then strengthens us to say 'no' in the Christian walk is the practice of the spiritual disciplines that can be seen in the practices of purging possessions, curbing the impulse to acquire, fasting, radical generosity and hospitality.

Summary

Jesus established the way things were to work in the kingdom. It is, in, by, and through the Holy Spirit. Through the Spirit is how we enter the kingdom and it needs to be how we continually operate within the kingdom; however, that is not always automatic. The spiritual disciplines will help in keeping the flesh at bay so your actions, visions, and understandings are of God and not yourself.

There can be a fleshly spirit resident in every organized institution (yes, Christian ones included). Your goal is to see that the spirit driving the establishment that you labor in is not of the flesh but the Holy Spirit. To do that you must live in the Spirit, be guided by the Spirit, and have evidence of the fruit of the Spirit. Recall the seven churches of Asia, six had a status quo that needed to be broken by the Spirit and one needed to continue to grow by the Spirit. Recall also that it took the Apostle John being in the Spirit to bring the spiritual instructions to their respective institutions.

Remember too the words of John the Baptist when faced with fleshly questions about Jesus' ministry outgrowing his:

"John answered and said, A man can receive nothing, except it be given him from heaven" (John 3:27). We are not in competition with others in the kingdom; and we are not a manufacturing plant where fleshly business models and assembly lines produce eternal results. The Kingdom of God is bucolic; it is sheep in the field and fruit on a tree, both requiring some of our time, care, and love, but both created by and ultimately dependent upon the Lord if they are to flourish.

Finally, you must always recognize the counter culture of the kingdom, as Jesus would say to the epitome of a worldly empire: "Jesus answered [Pilate], 'My kingdom is not of this world. If my kingdom were of this world, my servants would have been fighting, that I might not be delivered over to the Jews. But my kingdom is not from the world' (John 18:36 ESV). "The culture of the Kingdom is a backwards place where, as Jesus described, the 'first shall be last and the last first.' It's upside down. Backwards. Whatever 'empire' does, Kingdom does the opposite. The forgotten faces of an empire sit on the thrones of the kingdom".[18]

---

[16] Rood, Michael John, The Chronological Gospels (Fort Mill, SC: Aviv Moon Publishing, 2013).

[17] Wuest, Kenneth Samuel, Wuest's Word Studies from the Greek New Testament: For the English Reader, 3 vols. (Grand Rapids, Mich.: Eerdmans, 1973).

[18] Corey, Benjamin L., "5 Practices Toward A More Radical Christian Life," 5 Practices Toward A More Radical Christian Life, n.d., http://www.patheos.com/blogs/formerlyfundie/5-practices-toward-a-more-radical-christian-life/.

6—New Vision and Renewed Passion

"Lift up your eyes…" (John 4:35)

As He enters the last week of His first 100 days, two noteworthy changes take place in a single afternoon: He introduces a new vision to his disciples (John 4:21-23, 35), and a renewed and separating passion enters His work (v. 32-34).

New Vision

It had been around the halfway point of His first 100 days when Jesus had cleansed the Temple; that is, He had upended the status quo with the idea of returning the Temple to its original purpose. It was to be a house of prayer and a place of Presence. Now, six weeks later, He takes that original mission to the next level in a single conversation with a woman at a well: "Jesus saith unto her, Woman, believe me, the hour cometh, when ye shall neither in this mountain, nor yet at Jerusalem, worship the Father….But the hour cometh, and now is, when the true worshippers shall worship the Father in spirit and in truth: for the Father seeketh such to worship him" (John 4:21, 23).

We understand that the practical outworking of this new vision would take several years to accomplish as the Twelve would be sent, initially, to the lost sheep of the house of Israel. But with the Great Commission, the Day of Pentecost, Cornelius' Holy Spirit baptism, and the Jerusalem Council, the 'new' vision (though it truly was always His plan from the foundation of the world) would come to fruition.

Thus, the status quo vision of a 'closed' religion for only a few would give way to the new vision of a salvation for whomsoever will!

Renewed Passion

Notice too the personal change Jesus experienced following His conversation with the woman of Sychar. The scenario had begun with Jesus "being wearied with his journey" (John 4:6) and thirsty, "Give me to drink" (v. 7). It culminated with a rested fullness that testified, "Jesus saith unto them, My meat is to do the will of him that sent me, and to finish his work" (John 4:34). It was a fullness of such plentitude that the disciples thought someone else had provided a meal for the Master, "Therefore said the disciples one to another, Hath any man brought him ought to eat?" (v. 33).

I understand that the apparent weariness of the Lord that day was from His physical journey; however, I can't help but think He was also wearied in spirit as He chose to move the conversation from natural to spiritual water. For some weeks now He had been battling the status quo and personal persecution. He must have been tired in spirit as the Son of
52

Man, just as we get tired in spirit in our work from the constant resistance previously established by rote program. Sychar means 'drunken.' Thus, the woman of Sychar personified all who constantly refill their personal water pot and continually drink the apathy of ritual contained therein. But in her response to the living water, she left her jug—and all it exemplified—to embrace the life in Christ's living water. She was not the only one renewed—the Lord and His band, coupled with the town's residents, were all changed!

Summary

Notice all the positive changes that took place in the participants through the simple admonition to 'look up:' Jesus was personally renewed; the seed for the universal gospel was planted in the Twelve; and the hope of salvation was extended to a people who had no hope.

Rest assured the honeymoon environment in your new leadership position will not last forever. It will end and it could end very suddenly. It may have ended earlier when resistance flared against upending the status quo, or with a fleshly rebellion in moving to a modus operandi of the Spirit. Or you may have experienced a gradual ebbing of your honeymoon phase as those who couldn't embrace your leadership just quietly slipped away—or at least became sporadic attenders and unsupportive members, with you all the while feeling a subtle, dissatisfied undercurrent pulling them further out in the sea of apathy.

However, there are some who are staying with you. First there is your trustworthy core; then those who have been spiritually quickened by what's been accomplished thus far in your first 100 days. Their hope is renewed and it is time to put that hope into reality with a new vision for mission.

Returning to the original mission—salvation—in upending the status quo was just the first part of the missional equation. Once the return has been espoused then it must be 'customized' for your location by launching a new vision in practice. Jesus did just that with the woman at the well. He gave his disciples a whole new world to work with His command: "Say not ye, There are yet four months, and then cometh harvest? behold, I say unto you, Lift up your eyes, and look on the fields; for they are white already to harvest" (John 4:35).

Because His Word is life, a fresh Word is always uplifting; even more so when it gives direction and purpose. Hence Jesus' transition from being wearied and thirsty at the well to being renewed and full just a few minutes later with His disciples. Paul experienced the same in his new vision for the work in becoming the apostle to the Gentiles (cf. Acts 13:46) There is a confident liberty when you know you are doing God's perfect will for your life, and that new vision brings both confirmation and opportunity.

That opportunity is seen in a verse easily overlooked in this passage: "So when the Samaritans were come unto him, they besought him that he would tarry with them: and he abode there two days" (John 4:40). Those two days had to be so enjoyable to our Lord. After all the resistance in Jerusalem by the religionists of the day, here was a people group who embraced Him and listened. Implementing that new vision will do the same for you and give you an audience who wants to hear—so stay with them!

7—Reaffirmation

"So he came again to Cana in Galilee..."
(John 4:46).

Coming to the close of the Lord's first 100 days of ministry, He returns to the place of His first miracle. It was the place where His trustworthy selections had moved from believing in Him to trusting in Him (cf. John 2:11) as seen in Chapter Two. Only this time, the affirmation that God was with Him would be different. Let it be known that your affirmation will be different as well. This reaffirmation is not likely to be in the form of an immediate or visible sign. More likely, it will be a quiet event that must be carried to fruition by faith before it is evident.

Unless You See Signs and Wonders

For the first sign in Cana, in a response to His mother, Jesus opted for an immediate physical witness when He turned water into wine. Here however, at the behest of a father, Christ's witness was not one of sight, but of faith, as the man believed Jesus' words (cf. John 4:50) and witnessed it the next day. For His trustworthy ones, the miracle served a twofold purpose: 1) it reaffirmed that God was with Jesus; 2) it emphasized that faith was a necessary practice in ministry.

Moses and Joshua

This twofold purpose—the reaffirmation of God's anointing remaining resident in a leader and the necessity of faith in action—is excellently illustrated much earlier in scripture as seen in the Israelites' transition from Moses' leadership to Joshua's. The key verse in that transition is found in Joshua 5:12, "And the manna ceased the day after they ate of the produce of the land. And there was no longer manna for the people of Israel, but they ate of the fruit of the land of Canaan that year."

God had miraculously provided for Israel while in their wilderness wanderings with manna from heaven, but once they entered the promised land, once Joshua led them across the Red Sea and they began to fulfill the work God had called them to do in conquering the land—the manna ceased. Their 'food' would be living by faith in doing the work they were called to do. Similarly, at the establishing of your authority in this new position, there were sustaining signs (manna) that witnessed such early on. However, these early signs must give way to the work God has called you to do. By your inspiration, those you lead will witness the anointing in your word, their faith will rise, your authority will be reaffirmed, and the work will be everyone's sustenance—just as it was for those in Joshua's day.

The Father Knew

There is something here that is important to keep in mind. Just as the father confirmed the words of Jesus in the healing of his son the next day (cf. John 4:53), your reaffirmation is not going to be instantaneous. While your initial affirmation might have been as immediately manifest as manna in the morning, your reaffirmation is fruit of a more eventual harvest. It will come as those who choose to follow you by faith witness your shared inspiration in their work; and the Modus Operandi—the Holy Spirit—will bring it to their remembrance regardless of where they are located.

Summary

At the close of His first 100 days Jesus reaffirmed His authority with a miracle at Cana, only this time it wasn't instantaneous by turning water into wine. Rather, it would take a day and some 20 miles to validate. Firstly, there is a need for reaffirmation. Secondly, not every authority-establishing incident is immediate. Some will take time—and in that time faith is the backcloth to the work. But be it 20 miles later or 20 days later, the Holy Spirit will bring the words you spoke by inspiration back to those who heard them, and your authority will continue to be strengthened.

Following the sharing of a new vision there will need to be a reaffirmation that 'God is with you.' The spoken vision to 'lift up your eyes' to that which challenges—and then sees well beyond—the status quo necessitates a confirmation that the anointing still resides in you. Only this time, it won't be as dramatic as the first...or as quick. Rather, it will probably even be affirmed away from you—just as it was with the Master. A word you have spoken will come alive to those who heard sometime later (cf. 1 Peter 1:10-12) and your leadership will be affirmed.

That affirmation will come as those you lead exercise faithful service in their calling to fulfill God's mission for this particular people. Those you lead will make the transition from believers following signs to signs following believers as they are fed from the work of the ministry as inspired by your words and actions in the new mission.

In this finale, the Lord also lets us know that reaffirmation will be a continuing principle throughout your tenure—just as it was with him. The Lord's words came back to the Trustworthy many times: Peter's foretold denial (cf. Matthew 26:75); the Eleven following the resurrection (cf. Luke 24:8); and Peter in Cornelius' Holy Spirit baptism (cf. Acts 11:16). So too were the Trustworthy's words remembered as seen in Jude 17 and Acts 20:35. Be assured, your words as inspired of the Spirit and your leadership as led by the Lord will be called to remembrance as well!

And Why It Matters

When it comes to genuine ministry—ministry that is of the Spirit, for only the Spirit can minister in the eternal—so much is out of the pastor's control. Yet, pastors are the ones who carry the weight of a church's 'success.' Unrealistic expectations, so many times based on natural business models or the American dream of work harder to gain more (because bigger is always better they say), bury joy through burnout by slaying their spirit with the sword of frustration.

After reading a final draft of this book, a minster of some 30 plus years wrote: "Your words fed my soul and confirmed in me the many things that have happened and continue to happen in my ministry...your conclusion is right on. You nailed a primary need for every minister. The paramount need for patience while you allow God to do His work. Let God be God and the minister have patience as he is involved with what God is doing. God gives the increase. God builds the house. God holds up the faithful."

That is why the first 100 days matter. These seven principles are the foundation on which your leadership is built; however, being foundational does not mean they won't be revisited repeatedly—and not just in new positions. The fact is your foundation will be tested, strengthened, and built upon throughout each leadership opportunity. These seven principles need to be at the forefront of the pastor's understanding and prayerfully laid as the bedrock of any expectation.

Remember the Seven

1—Be True to Yourself in Christ

Know you will be tempted in body, soul, and spirit to do things your way rather than His.

2—Selecting Trustworthy Individuals

These are far from 'yes men' but people of integrity who see Christ in you and respect both His authority and those whom He delegates it to.

3—Establishing Spiritual Authority

So many times, establishing spiritual authority doesn't happen at a planned moment; rather, a sharing of an inspired word that speaks volumes to its hearer…and they know it's from the Lord.

4—Upending the Status Quo

Change isn't always easy, especially in the passionate environment of church. However, Spirit inspired transformation is all part of being changed from glory to glory.

5—Modus Operandi, The Holy Spirit

Always recognize the counter culture of the Kingdom and the need for the Holy Spirit every day.

6—New Vision and Renewed Passion

Constantly hearing from the Spirit will give you fresh and relevant vision that renews a passionate hope in ministry.

7—Reaffirmation

Living the life, seeing that the above principles are practiced and evident, will continue to bring a reaffirmation of your leadership to those who see Christ in you.

About the Author

Pastor John Pace accepted Christ in 1981 and has spent the past 33 years in full-time ministry His efforts in serving the Lord in denominational leadership with the Church of God of Prophecy (Cleveland, TN) took him to over 40 states and 40 countries around the world. Still, there is no place he would rather be than in the presence of the Lord and at Crimson House.

As the founding Pastor of Crimson House in 2001, Pastor John transplanted a fledgling local church on the outskirts of town into the heart of historic Springfield. It has now become a lively urban ministry center, with an active local body offering assistance and programs to over 750 non-congregants each month. His anointing to show people the love of Jesus and his laid-back teaching style create a culture of discipleship and belonging. One of his greatest rewards is to hear someone call Crimson House "home."

Pastor John attended Gordon-Conwell Theological Seminary. He enjoys spending time with his wonderful wife, Diane, and their seven beautiful children.

For more information on Crimson House see www.crimsonhouseministries.org

Additional books written by Pastor John can be found at the Crimson House Ministries curriculum outlet, Shepherds of the Lost, at www.shepherdsofthelost.org

www.ingramcontent.com/pod-product-compliance
Lightning Source LLC
Chambersburg PA
CBHW060038050426
42448CB00012B/3066